I0479727

FROM ZERO TO PROFIT:

The Ultimate Guide to Dominate Your Online Advertising.

Sam Austin

TABLE OF CONTENTS

Chapter 1

Introduction

Businesses can use Google Ads as a service to run advertisements and connect with customers who are prepared to buy. To reach the widest audience possible, the platform offers a variety of ad formats, such as display ads, video ads, search ads, and app ads. In other words, Google Ads is a platform for online advertising created by Google that allows advertisers to pay to display commercials, service offers video content, and encourages the download of mobile applications.

With Google Ads, advertisers can target relevant websites, remarket to particular audiences, place ads on various apps, and produce video ads that play before or alongside other pertinent videos. Google search is where search ads appear, whereas app ads can be displayed anywhere on the Google network, including inside other apps. Google Ads can be extremely effective at promoting and expanding a brand or company online due to the abundance of opportunities available. This is especially true for search advertising, where keywords can be targeted to speak directly to prospective clients.

PPC (pay-per-click) services are made available through Google Ads. With the pay-per-click (PPC) business model, businesses place their advertisements on websites and receive payments only when visitors click on them.

Facts About Google Advertising

1. There are 6.9 billion searches conducted on Google every day as of 2022, giving the company a 92% market share.

2. When making purchases, 65% of people click on advertisements.

3. The average "search" ad conversion rate across all industries is 4.40%.

4. Google has a 63% click-through rate, which is four times higher than that of any other ad network among online users.

How does Google advertising work?

Through targeted search, Google Ads can assist advertisers in bringing interested, pertinent customers to their websites. The procedure is easy. Google Ads will advertise in its search results when a user types in a word that is pertinent to or closely related to an advertiser's good or service. The goal is to reach users who are most likely to purchase a good or service. By providing a range of pricing options, advertisements also assist in managing and controlling the cost of advertising. Google Ads is a cost-effective option because advertisers only pay if a user clicks on an ad and visits a website.

Qualities of an Effective Google Ad.

Ad creation requires careful consideration of the best keywords to use. These are the key phrases that a potential customer will most likely use to find a company or product. Ads will be more likely to be seen by the most relevant audience by using relevant keywords and categorizing them.

Making an effective advertisement that captures attention quickly is also crucial. To get people to visit an advertiser's website, it must first speak to the audience in a way that makes sense to them.

Additionally, keep in mind that the landing page for an advertisement is the page a prospective customer will see after clicking the ad. A good landing page will answer the questions that the potential customer has.

Finally, Google Ads will display the number of users who saw an advertisement and clicked on it, whereas Google Analytics will display the duration of user engagement with an advertisement.

Why is Google advertising necessary?

1. To become more visible to a reputable audience

Google ads promote your goods or services to the appropriate market to encourage customers to take the action that is required of them.

2. To increase brand recognition

An efficient method of promoting your brand is through Google ads. According to Google research, "top-of-mind" awareness has increased. This is the concept of a brand or product being the first to enter a customer's mind when they consider a specific sector or category.

3. Retargeting website visitors

Retargeting lists for search ads (RLSA) and display network ads make it possible to target website visitors rather than customers who have already made a purchase.

Retargeting is the practice of going back to people you've already targeted but who didn't take the desired action. Then, to persuade them to act, you will retarget them or run your ads for them once more.

4. Enhancing intelligence

By using techniques like ECPC (Enhanced cost-per-click), bids for advertisements can be modified by previous conversion data and other details like device model, browser, etc.

5. Evaluating your ad performance

You can find out who clicked on your ads, how many leads were generated, how much traffic was directed to your website, and so much more with Google ads.

6. High flexibility

You can use Google Ads to target the audience you want to reach by using a variety of customization options (keyword selection, audience selection, etc.).

7. To assist with SEO (Search Engine Optimization)

As a result of the initial traffic, your website may rank higher on Google's search engine results page (SERP).

SERPs, or "search engine results pages," are the pages that search engines show in response to a query.

Chapter 2

Google Ads Hierarchy, Structure, Formats, and Campaign Objectives.

Hierarchy of Google Ads Campaign

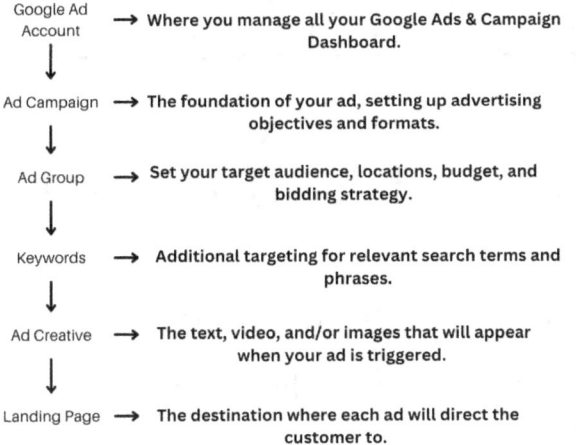

Google Ads Structure

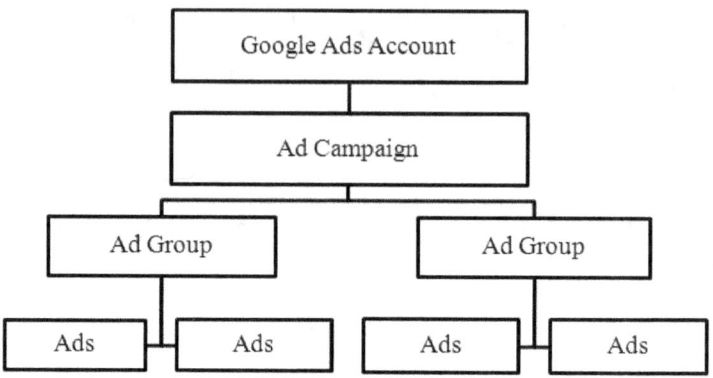

Google Adwords Campaign Formats and Types.

a. Search: With text ads, you can connect with customers who are interested in your goods or services.

b. Display: Run various online advertisements by gathering contact information, such as email addresses and other pertinent data.

c. Shopping: Use shopping ads to promote your products.

d. Video: Reach and interact with viewers on YouTube and the internet.

e. App: Promote apps across Google's networks.

f. Smart: Reach your business objectives with automated ads on Google and other websites.

g. Local: Encourage customers to visit a physical location.

h. Discovery: Run advertisements on Discover, Gmail, YouTube, and other sites.

Campaign Objectives and Their Features for Google Ads

a. Sales: Increase sales in-store, through phones, in apps, and online. [Campaign types: video, search, shopping, display, smart, and discovery].

b. Leads: Encourage customers to take action to generate leads and other conversions. [Campaign types: video, shopping, display, smart, search, and Discovery].

c. Website Traffic: Entice the right audience to visit your website. [Campaign types: video, shopping, display, search, and discovery].

d. Product and Brand Consideration: Encourage people to learn more about your goods or services. [campaign type: video].

e. Brand Awareness and Reach: Reach a large audience and increase awareness [campaign types: display and video].

f. App Promotion: Increase the number of app downloads, interactions, and pre-registrations. [campaign type: App].

g. Local Store Visits and Promotions: Drive customers to local businesses, such as restaurants and auto dealerships. [campaign type: Local].

h. Create a Campaign Without a Goal's Guidance: With no recommendations based on your goal, pick a campaign type first.

Chapter 3

Google Ads Campaign

Let me explain how Google Ads operates before I start discussing best practices for managing a successful Google Ads campaign. This is the relevant result that Google will display if I enter "website developer" as my search term.

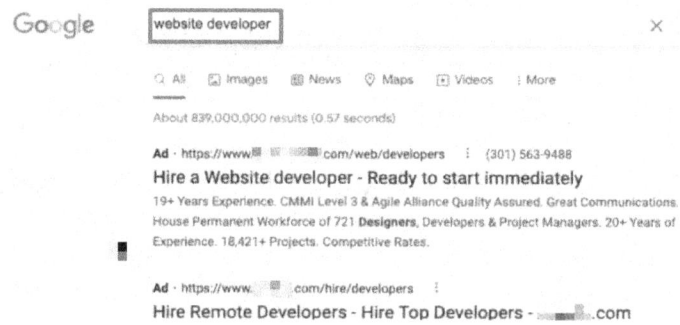

Google is taking advantage of its position and ability to organize the data in such a way that it is giving every advertiser the option to pay and pair for any search terms. The ad appears in front of the URL in the search term above, serving as an illustration of ads.

The following image serves as an illustration of organic search results; these listings did not pay to be on the first page for the keyword "website developer".

The steps outlined in the procedure that follows will show you how to use Google ads to show up in the search results for particular keywords that will result in more clients. As a result, Google charges for each click that results from people seeing that advertisement. Because of this, it is referred to as "pay-per-click" (PPC) advertising.

❖ To manage a single account, enter "ads.google.com" into Google. You will end up on a part of the page like this.

Grow your business with Google Ads

Get in front of customers when they're searching for businesses like yours on Google Search and Maps. Only pay for results, like clicks to your website or calls to your business.

To help you get started with Google Ads, we'll give you $500 in free ad credit when you spend $500.

Start now

Just enter "MCC account" in the Google search box if you want to manage clients' multiple accounts. MCC stands for "Google My Client Center."

❖ Create a Google Ads account by clicking "start now" or logging in with your Gmail account on Google.

Google

Sign in

to continue to Google Ads

Email or phone

Forgot email?

Not your computer? Use Guest mode to sign in privately.
Learn more

Create account   Next

You can sign in with your current Google account or create a new account—which need not be a Gmail address—if you prefer.

❖ After logging in, a new page will appear with four options; instead of choosing any of them, scroll down and select "Switch to Expert Mode."

If, after logging in, you are unable to see "switch to expert mode," Typically, it occurs while using a mobile device. Simply remove "/express" from your URL link so that when you click ENTER after doing so, you are taken to the expert mode page.

❖ You can select your campaign objective on the expert mode page. I'll go with "create a campaign without a goal's guidance."

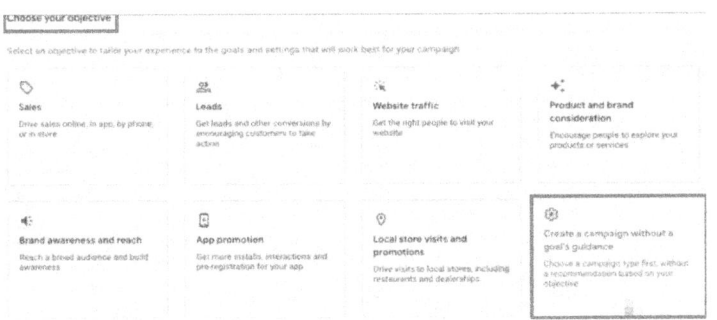

❖ You will choose the type of campaign you want to create. For a beginner, I will recommend you select "search"

❖ The three options are website visits, phone calls, and app downloads, and you can select any of them. Select none of them, then click the "Continue" button.

❖ Name your campaign: I'll be creating a campaign for a website designer who is using Google ads to find more clients.

General settings

Type: Search

Campaign name

Search Campaign (Website Design)

❖ Deselecting the two networks will prevent you from being charged by Google in this additional way. You will undoubtedly be charged if you choose "Display Network," as Google will display your advertisement on other networks such as YouTube.

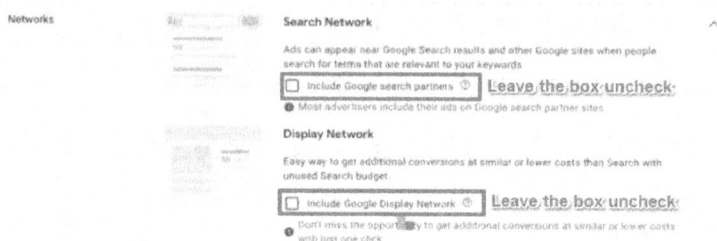

❖ Then, click on "show more settings."

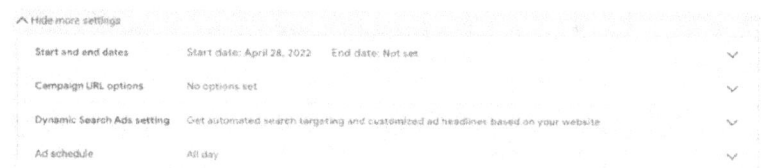

➢ **Start and end dates**: You can choose the ideal time or extension date for your ads. I'll only include the start date because I'll occasionally check on the status of my advertisement. The Dynamic Search Ads settings and campaign URL options can be ignored.

➤ **Ad Schedule**: If you want people to call you or come into your local store, this will be acceptable for you. Leave it set to "All day" if you want it available 24/7.

❖ The location of your customers should be determined under "targeting and audience segments." Choose the precise area where your target audience is. You can include or exclude your preferred location(s) by choosing "enter another location" and "advanced search" to focus your search. I decided on New York in the USA.

Additionally, click the location option and choose both the target and exclude options, as shown in the image presentation.

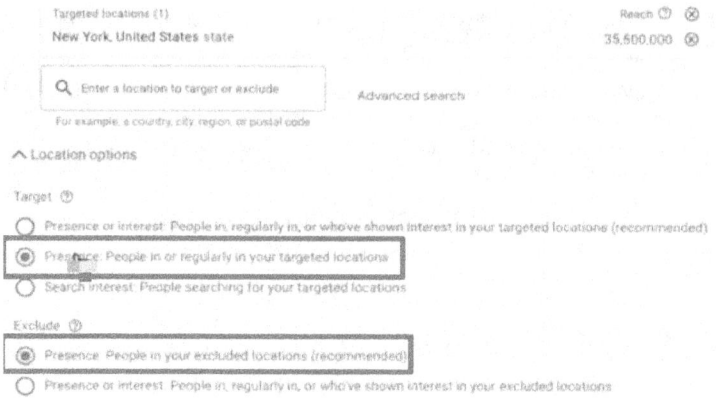

❖ You will undoubtedly use the language of your clients when it comes to languages. Skip the audience segments.

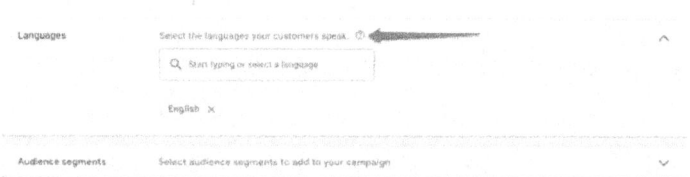

❖ Choose the currency you want to use to pay Google from the Budget and Bidding section. In addition, I set my daily budget average at $10.00.

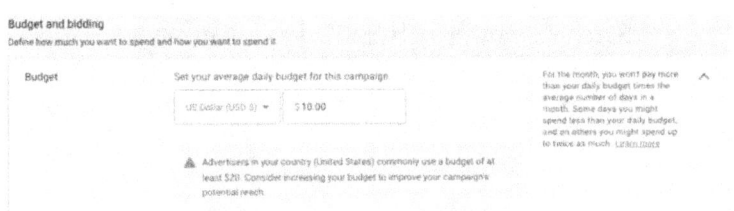

When it comes to bidding, I will advise you to click on "select a bid strategy directly (not recommended)" because Google won't want to help you make that choice and will also use that as an excuse to charge you more.

Next, choose manual CPC to give yourself more options for ad optimization by allowing you to customize every single ad and set the highest CPC you're willing to pay.

❖ Regarding ad extensions, I'll advise you to set them up because they will make your ad larger and increase your CTR. To get you through, pay attention to Google Ads' most significant extensions.

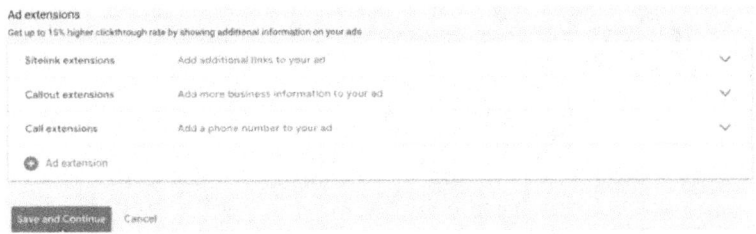

The four most crucial extensions for Google Ads campaigns

> **Sitelink Extension**: This kind of extension directs visitors to particular web pages on your site. For instance, when someone clicks on a link to a specific product or store, they are taken directly to the landing page, where they can learn more or make a purchase. Your CTR can rise by up to 50% on branded terms and by about 20–25% on unbranded terms when you use Sitelink extensions.

➢ **Callout Extension**: This gives you the option to highlight free shipping, discounts, price matching, and other offers in more detail in your advertisement. Unlike SiteLink, this extension does not include a link. Customers are always intrigued by it. Five-star ratings, handcrafted perfection, free delivery, a 100% money-back guarantee, durable quality, etc. are a few examples.

➤ **Call Extension**: This extension enables you to include phone numbers in your ads, which can significantly increase CTR. People can tap or click a button to call your company directly when your call extensions appear, increasing customer engagement with your ads and giving you more opportunities to capture and track conversions.

➢ **Location Extension**: Along with your ad text, you can display a company address, phone number, or map marker. By displaying your ads with your address, a map of your location, or the driving time to your establishment, Google Ads location extensions assist users in finding your locations.

New Homes From $200's - $500's | Orlando New Homes
[Ad] www.khov.com/New-Homes/Orlando ▾
New Homes From $200's - $500's. Devoted To Building Communities Of Excellence!
⚲ 1896 Ibis Bay Ct, Ocoee, FL · Closing soon · 10.00 AM – 6.00 PM ▾

❖ Next, on the Ad group level

➢ **Ad Group Name**: Here, I will be focusing on people who design WordPress websites. That is why I called my ad group "Website + WordPress."

➢ **Default Bid**: What you bid for your campaign will depend on the industry you are in. It merely means how much you're willing to pay per click.

Ad group name

Website + Wordpress

Default bid ⑦

$ 2

➢ **Keywords**: You must research the keywords you want your advertisement to appear for. There are a variety of methods for discovering keywords, and in this book, I'll outline how to use Google Keyword Planner.

You can enter the URL of your website or the names of your goods or services in the corresponding field. Google will look for keywords that are related to what you typed in the field. For instance, if a user searches for "WordPress website designer"

Keywords

Find relevant keywords by describing what you're advertising in this ad group

Enter related web page URL

wordpress website designer ✕   Add products or services

Get keywords

Then, click the "Get Keywords" button, and Google will bring up all associated keyword searches.

Choose between exact, phrase, and broad match keywords. I advise you to use phrase match and exact match keywords. While the phrase always appears in quotation marks, the exact match always appears in square brackets.

Google Adwords Keyword Match Types

Match Type	Special Symbol	Example Keyword	Ads may show on searches that	Example Searches
Broad Match	None	Women's hats	includes misspellings, synonyms, related searches, and other relevant variations	buy ladies hats
Phrase Match	"Keyword"	"Women's hats"	are phrases or close variations of that phrase.	buy women's hats
Exact Match	[Keyword]	[Women's hats]	are an exact term, and close variation of that exact terms	Women's hats

It will be a little stressful to add quotation marks and square brackets to your keywords, but there is a free website that does that. Just enter the name of the tool—Keyword Match Type Tool—into Google.

I'll copy and paste the keywords I came up with earlier onto the website. Select what you see inside the image when it appears like this.

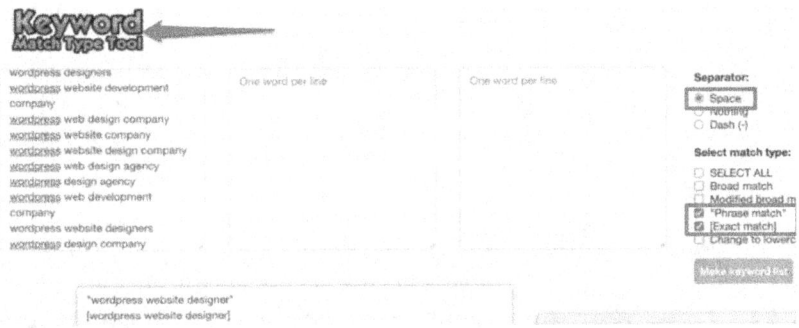

Recopy the new keywords, enclose them in quotation marks, and then paste them back into the keyword field.

You can create a new ad group, but make sure to fill it with between 20 and 25 keywords. To increase the likelihood that your advertisement will appear on the first page, especially when people are searching, make sure you test each keyword separately on Google to see how it performs and whether it appears on the first page. Click on "Save and Continue."

❖ You will then create an ad for the ad group you've created. You'll see the ad group with the keywords you created at the top.

Create ads

For each ad group, we recommend you create a responsive search ad with at least 'Good' ad strength that closely relates to the theme of your keywords.

Ad group: Website • Wordpress
Search Campaign (Website Design)

Keywords: wordpress website designer, wordpress website designer, wordpress website developer, wordpress website developer, wordpress web developer, wordpress web developer, wordpress designers + *5 more ✓ Show more

➤ **Final URL**: Suppose I have a landing page that I want visitors who are looking for website designers to access, specifically the destination page where I want visitors to take action.

➤ **Display Path**: Before they click on your ad, people see a display path like this: I advise you to use any of the powerful keywords you are aiming for. For Paths 1 and 2, I will use Web Developer and WordPress, respectively, because they are pertinent to what people are looking for. Additionally, they will award a high quality and relevancy score.

Final URL ⑦

https://websitedesigner.com/services

Required

Display path ⑦

websitedesigner.com / | web-developer | / | wordpress |

13 / 15   9 / 15

➢ **Headlines**: Make sure your headlines accurately reflect the search terms you want to rank for. Pay attention to the rules for appropriate headlines.

Headline 1: You must include keywords and let them reflect what your business entails. People will know they are in the right place if that is what they see.

Headline 2: Let it be CTA-focused. For instance, call for a free consultation and a 100% money-back guarantee.

Headline 3: Make a deal. Examples include receiving your free guide, working with athletes who are professionals, receiving unlimited revisions, and saving time and money. To write effective headlines, you must understand your audience.

To prevent Google from rotating the position of each headline, you can pin it where you want it to appear when someone searches.

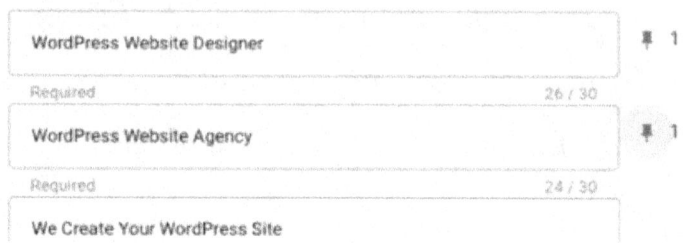

WordPress Website Designer   📌 1

Required   26 / 30

WordPress Website Agency   📌 1

Required   24 / 30

We Create Your WordPress Site

➢ **Descriptions**: People won't read the description; they will only skim it, so don't waste too much time on it. I do, however, advise that you include pertinent keywords. Utilizing nearly all of the available 90 characters is also crucial because doing so will make your ad larger, which will raise the CTR. then click the "Done" button.

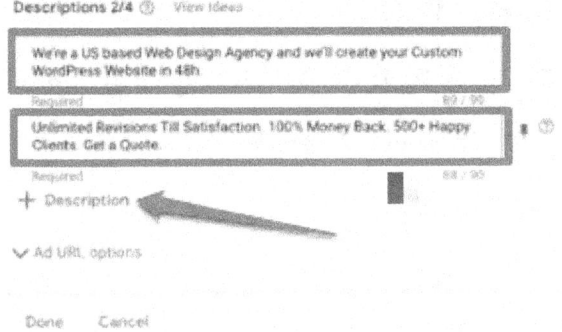

The next step is to click the "save and continue" button because I have finished creating my campaign's first group and am finished with my ad.

Ad group: Website + Wordpress
Search Campaign (Website Design)

Keywords: wordpress website designer, wordpress website designer, wordpress web developer, wordpress web developer, wordpress designers + 19 more

Ad · websitedesigner.com/web-develop...
WordPress Website Designer | WordPre...
We're a US based Web Design Agency a...
Unlimited Revisions Till Satisfaction. 10...

Save and continue

> **Setup Billing**: Enter the details of the credit card that will be used to pay for the Google advertisement. when you've finished it.

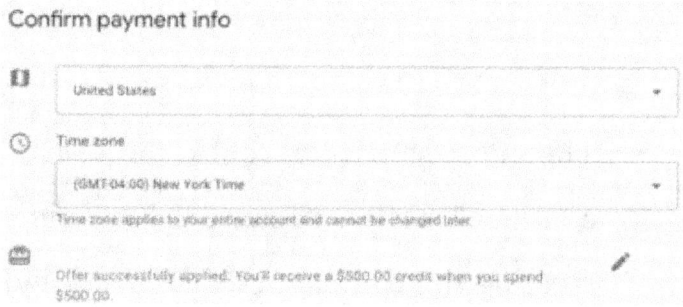

Click on the "Explore your campaign" button. You will then be automatically redirected to your Google Ads dashboard.

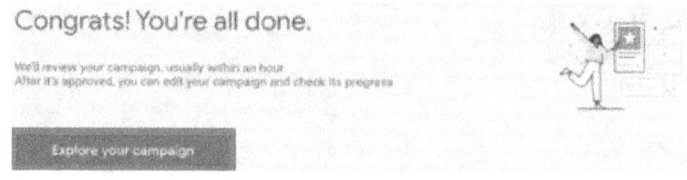

How to find Profitable Keywords using Google Keyword Planner

To match your ads to the terms people are searching for, you must use keywords, which are words or phrases. You can help your advertising campaign reach the target audience by choosing relevant, high-quality keywords.

I'll be outlining how to use Google Keyword Planner when creating your Google ads.

❖ Go to "tools and settings" in the top-right corner of your Google campaign dashboard, click it, and then choose "Keyword Planner."

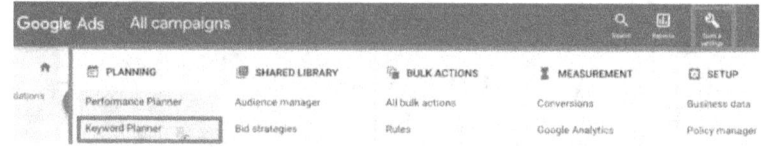

- ❖ There are two options in the keyword planner;

- ➢ **Discover new Keywords**: It can be used to simply connect with people who are interested in your goods or services.

- ➢ **Get Searched volume and Forecasts**: It can be used by agencies to calculate how much a new campaign will cost a client. I will select "Discover new Keywords."

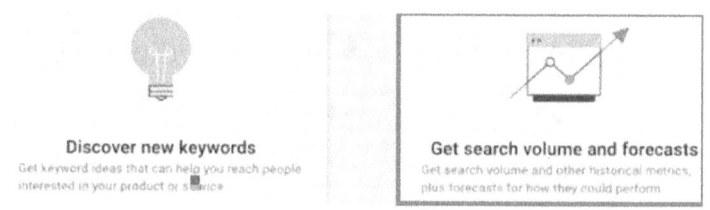

Discover new keywords
Get keyword ideas that can help you reach people interested in your product or service

Get search volume and forecasts
Get search volume and other historical metrics, plus forecasts for how they could perform

❖ Here, you can choose whether to "start with keywords" or "start with a website." By typing the URL of a popular website in your niche or one of your competitors' websites when selecting "start with website," Google will provide you with a bunch of information about potential keyword ideas.

The objective here is to obtain every possible keyword because you have to be extremely broad. Suppose I'm promoting a Facebook advertising agency while running a service-based business.

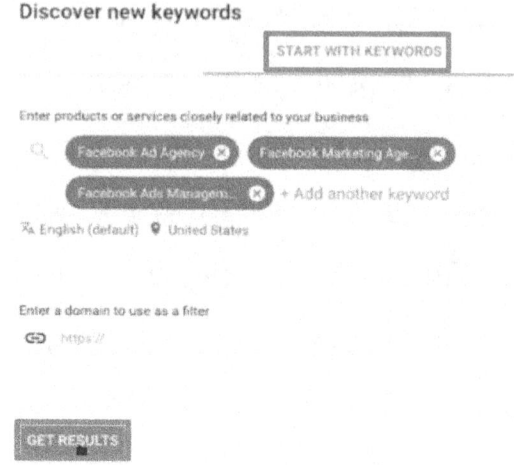

❖ The top of the page allows you to change the language and location. Be concise; in other words, select the country you want to target and obtain the entire keyword for that country. Additionally, you can filter your keyword results.

❖ It is preferable to refine keywords, which can be found in the right-hand corner. This will save you a ton of time, which is very helpful if you work in e-commerce. When you select "Expand All," some information that Google thinks you might not want to use in your search will be displayed. As you deselect some brand names or words, the number of potential keywords you can search for will decrease.

❖ Choose the most pertinent keywords from your list of search ideas that, to be more precise, represent someone looking for a Facebook advertising agency or service. Simply click "Add keywords to create a plan" after you have chosen your pertinent keywords. Your chosen keywords will appear as "In plan, saved."

27 selected	Plan ▾	New ad group ▾	Broad match ▾	Add keywords to create plan		
☐ Keyword (by relevance)				Avg. monthly searches	Three month change	YoY change
☐ digital marketing in facebook				100 - 1K	0%	0%
☐ add agency to facebook page				10 - 100	0%	0%
☑ facebook marketing agency for small business				10 - 100	0%	0%
☑ digital marketing agency facebook ads				10 - 100	0%	0%

❖ Then, on the left side, select "Keyword Plan" from the drop-down menu under "Keyword Ideas."

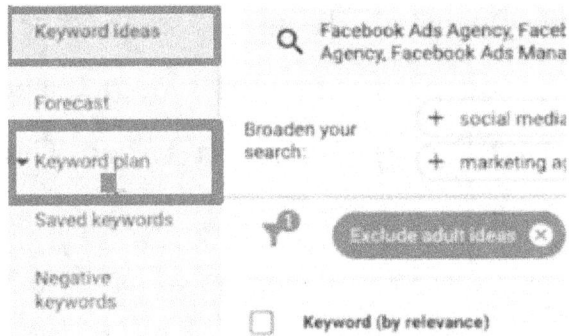

❖ You can view all of your saved keywords in the Keyword Plan. Choose your preferred options by clicking the download button. I'll download it as a CSV.

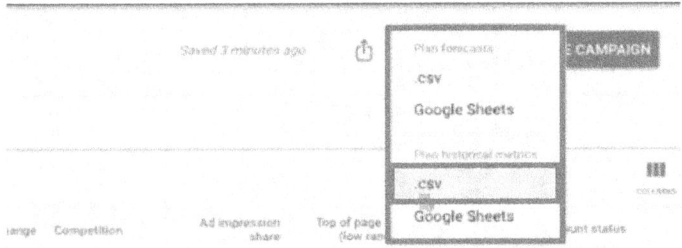

❖ Open the file in any spreadsheet program you prefer, such as Google Sheets, Open Office, or Microsoft Excel. They can be divided up into various ad group categories. Here is how I use the ad groups I've made to build a campaign.

Best Agency
best facebook ad agency
best facebook advertising agency
top facebook ad agencies

FB Ads Agency
facebook agency
advertising agency facebook
fb advertising agency
facebook ad agency near me

FB Marketing Agency
digital marketing agency facebook
digital marketing agency facebook ads
facebook marketing agency near me
marketing agency facebook
marketing agency facebook ads
social media marketing agency facebook ads

Company
facebook advertising company
facebook ads company
facebook marketing company

❖ Return to Keyword Ideas and select "Negative Keywords." By doing this, you are instructing Google that you do not want this keyword to appear whenever someone searches for your ad campaign. Keywords such as "free," "cheap," etc.

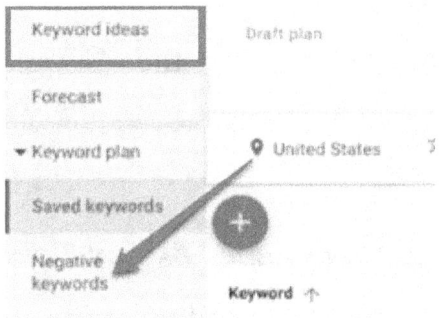

Chapter 4

Google Responsive Display Ads

The responsive ad for display automatically modifies its size, style, and format to fit available ad spaces on the Google Display Network.

Advantages of Google Display Network

1. It provides advanced targeting.

With "lookalike audiences" that can be made based on the audience you typically advertise to, you can target people who didn't interact with previous campaigns and reach out to new people.

2. Starting costs are comparatively low.

Running display ads is relatively inexpensive when compared to other forms of advertising like TV and radio.

3. It carries out advanced tracking.

It will assist in figuring out how frequently your advertisement was shown, clicked, and other factors.

4. The capacity to promote your brands to a larger audience.

The Google Display Network contains more than two million websites. This can greatly expand the audience for and exposure to your advertisements.

5. It increases interest in your product.

Your product will become more popular with appealing advertisements. The visibility and exposure that are necessary to make this possible are provided by the Google Display Network.

6. It increases website traffic.

7. It offers a wide variety of formats.

Display ads are more visually appealing and have the option of being animated, in contrast to search-only text-based ads. These offer higher click-through and conversion rates.

8. It remarkets your goods and services.

Users who have previously visited your website can see your ads by using retargeting or remarketing.

Differences between Google Display Network and Google Search Network

Google Display Network	Google Search Network
It works best for bottom-of-funnel activities like brand awareness. Users who may not be actively looking to buy but are merely researching see these ads.	It works best for top-of-funnel sales activities because customers are actively looking for the services and goods you offer.
Products that don't fill an immediate need are easier to advertise.	Products and services typically satisfy a specific need of the users.
You can use it to introduce users to your brand.	Ads are displayed to users based on their search terms.

Over a million websites display these ads to users.	Ads are displayed to users in Google services and apps.
Ads come in a variety of formats, including text ads, image ads, rich media ads, and video ads.	Ads are text-only.

Important metrics to track in Google Ads

1. Impression

These are the instances where your ad has appeared on a search result page via Google or the Google network.

2. Cost

These speak to the amount of money you have invested in your campaign.

3. Average Cost Per Click (CPC)

This is the typical cost per click from your campaign. i.e:

$$CPC = \frac{Cost}{Number\ of\ Clicks}$$

4. Conversion

These are added when a user clicks on your advertisement and completes an action you've defined as a goal (visiting the website, purchasing a good, etc.)

5. Cost Per Conversion

This is the typical price for conversions from your campaign. i.e:

$$Cost\ Per\ Conversion = \frac{Cost}{Number\ of\ Clicks}$$

6. Click-Through-Rate (CTR)

This is the proportion of clicks to impressions for your ads.

$$CTR = \frac{Total\ number\ of\ Clicks}{Total\ number\ of\ Impressions}$$

7. Quality Score

Google rates the effectiveness of your ads, keywords, and landing pages using this metric. It is reputed to be the foundation of Google ads.

★ Note: *Optimize your advertisement if you don't have a good quality score.*

Ways to improve your Google Ads

1. To boost click-through rates, include a call, review, or price extension in your ads.

2. To compel users to take immediate action, add a sense of urgency to your ad copy.

3. To ascertain which ad variant performs the best for you, split-test your ads.

4. To persuade your audience to take a specific action, including a call to action in your advertisements.

5. For maximum effectiveness, place your ads at the top of the page.

6. If your business has a physical location, optimize for local searches. Utilize the extension to show a thumbnail map of your location.

7. Make sure your advertising is running when your target audience is online.

8. Make sure some of your advertisements take advantage of celebrations, holidays, and other events.

9. If your ads must appear at a specific time, choose the accelerated delivery method, which uses up your daily budget more quickly.

10. Before creating your ad, conduct thorough keyword research.

11. Use negative keywords to make sure no one who searches for those unrelated terms sees your ads.

12. Improve your quality score, CTR, and message matching by using dynamic keyword insertions.

13. To generate leads and raise CTR rates, use branded keywords.

14. To limit which Google searches can activate your ads, use broad matching, phrase match, and exact match.

15. Make sure your quality score stays between 7 and 10. Your efforts will be

rewarded by Google with improved results and lower CPC.

16. Make sure your landing pages are responsive to mobile devices.

17. Your keywords should be grouped and organized to help you create ad groups with better landing pages, relevant text ads, and quality scores.

18. To target your ads, organize your campaigns and ad groups.

19. Spend more money on keywords that are converting rather than those that aren't.

20. To get the best results, use automatic bidding for ads.

Chapter 5

The Pros and Cons of using Google Advertisements

Let's begin with Google Ads' advantages. The advantages of utilizing Google ads include the following:

1. Quick Results.

The ability of Google Ads to produce immediate results is the first advantage to recognize. This is important because it can take months or even years to scale up many other traffic generation techniques like content creation, blogging, and social media.

Because Google Ads make use of the way Google is set up, they can produce results immediately. Google displays ads at the top and on the sides of your screen when you search. They'll grab the viewer's attention because they're frequently extremely relevant to what you were looking for, which will then drive traffic to your website where you can make sales, gather subscribers, or generate leads.

2. Possibility of Testing & Experimenting. With Google Ads, you can quickly test what works and what doesn't. The second benefit of using Google Ads is its quick testing capability. Since not all experiments are the same, they will all produce unique results. For instance, you might experiment with running an advertising campaign for a particular set of service-related keywords one month, and then switch it up the following month by running advertisements for a different service. These two experiments will

produce different results, even with the same audience, because, most likely, various people prefer to purchase various services. With Google Ads, you can easily access split-testing tools like Google Optimize and quickly identify what works through testing. You might be able to avoid months or years of trial and error all at once by doing this.

3. Measure Results

You have an unrivaled ability to measure your results with Google Ads. You can use the dashboard to assess the performance of each advertising campaign. You'll be able to see which search terms are producing the best results, when the most click-throughs occur during the day, which particular ads are converting the best, etc.

4. Flexible Advertising Budgets

We adore Google Ads because it eliminates the need for a sizable advertising budget, as there once was with mass media advertising. Because Google Ads are pay-per-click, you only need to decide how much you want to spend; once you've reached that amount, the system will automatically stop running your ads.

For instance, if you set a budget of $50 per day, your ad won't run if it doesn't generate $50 or more in clicks per day. Your ad will only run while it generates enough conversions to reach $50 per day, even if it is receiving a ton of traffic but no conversions just yet. By doing this, new businesses can continue to build their brand without having to wait years for profits.

5. Possibility of High ROI

With Google Ads, any advertiser who is worth their salt should be able to produce a 2x return on ad spend (ROAS). Finding out how many conversions you receive for each dollar spent is made simple by Google. In terms of return on advertising spend, Google Ads outperforms other traffic generation strategies, according to the statistics, which show that the average ROAS with Google Ads is between 4x and 5x, but the majority of advertisers anticipate 2x in their first year.

6. Targeted Advertising

In the past, it was nearly impossible to target your advertising; you might be able to pick a TV station, a particular radio program, or a neighborhood to send flyers to. You can target people based on their location, interests, keywords, time of day, age, type of device, and a lot more using Google Ads (and other PPC) advertising platforms.

You can cut costs and only advertise to people who are interested in your goods or services by using hyper-targeted advertisements.

7. Broad Geographical Reach

By letting you select which regions, cities, or countries to limit your ads to, Google Ads gives you a geographically diverse reach. It enables you to do that if you only want your advertisement to appear in the USA and nowhere else. Due to this, businesses in smaller markets or nearby cities can easily have an impact on the audiences that are important to them.

8. Cost Per Click (CPC)

Another benefit is that you can pay per click. This payment method is incredibly beneficial, especially for small service businesses. When someone views your ad on many other platforms, such as Facebook, you will typically be charged (committed per thousand impressions, or CPM payments). You only pay with CPC payments when a user clicks on your advertisement and is directed to your landing page. This implies that you are only paid when a customer views your service offering.

9. High Intent Users

Google is an effective advertising platform because of the motivation behind its users. Users who search on Google, in contrast to most social media users, are actively trying to find a solution. Consider yourself as an illustration:

You most likely found this blog via a search engine because you are actively attempting to determine whether Google ads are worthwhile for your company. If you decide that Google Ads are worthwhile, you'll need to decide whether you want to set them up on your own or if you want to hire a marketing company.

You came across this article because you are driven to find a solution to a problem. Your customers are the same way. They are searching Google for solutions to their issues. When you advertise on Google, you're reaching hundreds or thousands of buyers who are motivated to buy!

10. Ability to remarket
You can use Google Ads to display your advertisements to website visitors who have

already been there but have not yet converted. This is known as remarketing, and it's a fantastic way to remind people of all the goods and services they abandoned but are now willing to provide once more. Although it's not always best to start with remarketing ads, they can be very effective when done right.

I've discussed some advantages of using Google Ads; now, I'll list and discuss some drawbacks. The drawbacks include the following:

11. Single and Inactive

Like any advertising system, the ads are useless on their own because the website's navigation and landing pages are what persuade potential customers to make a purchase. Users won't purchase anything from you if they think your website is difficult to use, unreliable, or frustrating.

This implies that you can have a perfectly curated ad account and still not make any sales. Before launching your ads, it's critical to comprehend how to build a comprehensive marketing system. The majority of companies get stuck here. If this sounds like a lot of work, you might want to research marketing companies that can help you get started with a thorough advertising system.

12. Possibility of High CPC

If you don't have a large company's marketing budget, it may be difficult to profit from your clicks in highly competitive industries because of the high cost per click.

Having said that, many industries with high cost per click can defend it because their goods or services have a very high price. The education sector is an example. Spending $50 or even $100 per click might be acceptable if a college student is going to spend $50,000 a year or even more on education.

But you'll probably be exempt from this. If your Google Ads account is properly configured, the average cost per click for most service businesses will fall between $1.50 and $3, typically closer to the lower end of that range.

13. Setting details

Google Ads can be very complicated for people who have never used PPC before. You can choose to turn it on or off, or set many different settings. These options are crucial for optimization, but if you don't understand what they each do, they could be very confusing. Conversion tracking is one of those settings that, if set up incorrectly, can render the data and ads in your account completely useless.

14. Time Commitment

Even for seasoned users, Google Ads can take a lot of time, like anything that yields results. If you find that this is a problem, you might want to appoint a specific employee to manage all of your digital marketing. Many times, hiring a marketing agency is less expensive.

15. Data purchasing

While Google Ads can create a profile fairly quickly (in the first few months of operation), they are much more capable after a year or more of active optimization and testing.

You are essentially purchasing the data that will be necessary to properly optimize the account in the early stages of your advertising. The data you buy in advance is what will allow you to produce a 3x–5x ROAS.

16. Keyword intent

Due to their lack of understanding of keyword intent, those who have no prior experience with digital marketing frequently find themselves blowing a lot of money on their Google Ads accounts.

You will continuously overpay for clicks that yield scant or no results if you don't understand how people search and what kinds of goods or services they expect to see when they do so. Unfortunately, unless you've been investing money in the account for a while and have enough conversion tracking set up to gather this data, it can be very challenging to get accurate data on your keywords.

This implies that you will have already spent a fair amount of money by the time you have a sufficient amount of data to realize you are not getting any results. Before you start advertising, be sure you know what you're trying to achieve.

17. Emotional Effects

Human emotion is yet another drawback of Google advertising. Many business owners are unsure whether the cost of advertising is appropriate for them, and once they start to feel the cost, they stop advertising. When you start your advertising campaign, be careful not to overextend.

This is a risky strategy because it can significantly reduce the amount of potential business you can generate and waste all of the time, resources, and money you put into creating your advertising campaigns. Make sure you are comfortable with the numbers and fully understand the start-up costs before you begin working with an advertising agency.

Google Tag Manager, Google Ads Conversion Tracking, Google Analytics, and Google Analytics 4

Chapter 6

Google Tag Manager (GTM)

This Google tool is available for free and can be used by any marketer to deploy and monitor tags on their website. In other words, it's a tag management system that makes it possible to quickly and easily update measurement codes and related code fragments, also known as tags, on your website or mobile app. The following are examples of tags that can be used with Google Tag Manager:

a. Google Analytics

b. Facebook Pixel

c. Google Adwords

How does Google Tag Manager operate?

Google Tag Manager has a container tag that can be added to your website pages. This eliminates the requirement for using numerous different codes on a website. Since the same code is used on all pages, a site's individual pages don't require rewriting. You can also use this tool to monitor activity on your mobile apps. All you have to do is use the Firebase SDK for iOS or Android. You can use GTM to have tags automatically updated on your site without having to put in the time-consuming work of manually coding them.

You aren't constrained by the number of tags you are managing at once because you can tag more than one website at once. This makes it incredibly simple, especially if you manage multiple websites. Be aware that you will need a separate account for each company, even if you work on multiple websites or other businesses.

To connect to Google Tag Manager, you simply need to insert a few lines of code into your website or application. When this occurs, a web-based interface will work to automatically add the codes to your page. The triggers on the interface can be selected by the person running the tag manager.

The trigger will activate when something takes place. Events include things like "page loads," "a user taps on the screen," "selecting an option," or clicking "submit" on any forms you have on your website. GTM activates in response to the event, collects the data, and then sends it back to Google Analytics. Furthermore, it will help you manage the tags on your website so you don't have to put in the extra effort.

The advantages of Google Tag Manager

1. Rapid code deployment and testing
2. Every tag is managed in one location.
3. A simple version control method
4. Auto event tracking capability, which monitors various website buttons
5. It is completely free
6. Extremely secure

Components of Google Tag Manager

Google Tag Manager is composed of three main parts, namely:

1. Tags

They are permitted to control actions like scroll tracking, remarketing, total clicks, file downloads, clicks on particular links, etc. JavaScript code installation is its primary purpose. Unless you use a tag manager, tags must be added to each page of your website. The component that monitors what occurs on each of your web pages is the tag. The tags can determine how visitors are utilizing the features on your website.

They are useful when combined with a program like Google Tag Manager because they can track the data you require and want automatically. The code is added to GTM, which aids in tracking the data you require. The tags will consequently appear automatically on each of your web pages.

The tag manager also has a fantastic feature that can alert you when your code isn't functioning. This makes it simple for you to understand what needs to be done to return to the tag manager and fix the code. A problem could not be solved if it was not obvious that it existed.

2. Trigger

It is an essential component of a container. It also acts as a factor in determining whether or not a tag should be fired. A trigger must exist before a tag can be created. Events that take place on the page are called triggers, and when they do, tags will activate. This implies that the data will be gathered from the tag and stored wherever you choose.

This is why integrating your GTM with Google Analytics is a good idea. A webmaster can choose from a wide variety of triggers to gather information. Triggers can occur when a user accesses certain pages of a website, clicks on buttons, scrolls down for more details, or downloads something. When forms are filled out or purchases are made, that may also count. These are merely a few examples, but Google Tag Manager offers a wide variety of trigger options.

3. Variables

When defining a trigger or sending data to tags, it stores the information. It includes various types of information, such as the product name, product value, or date. Additionally, variables can transmit very specific information. When a visitor clicks on a link, you can either specify variables or choose to include all click types. This will enable all of the various variable options to remain available. If you want to keep track of specific actions, like clicks on a particular URL, use variables. It's crucial to determine the values required for the various variables you want to track. The rate at which a user scrolls up or down on a page, the quantity of what they have purchased, or the amount of time they have spent on a particular page of your website are some examples of variables.

These factors can help you keep track of the information that is most important and relevant for marketing or usability requirements. To obtain the most precise information, variables are used with both triggers and tags. To ensure that you receive the information you need when you need it, it can be helpful to exclude irrelevant data.

How to set up your Google Tag Manager account

❖ Enter "Google Tag Manager" into the search bar to get started; on a PC, you'll see a page similar to this one; click the "start for free" button. If you're using a mobile device, click "Create account" to continue.

❖ You'll be directed to your administrative dashboard. Fill in the following fields:

➢ **Account Setup**: Enter the names of your country and company. Uncheck "Share data anonymously with Google and others"

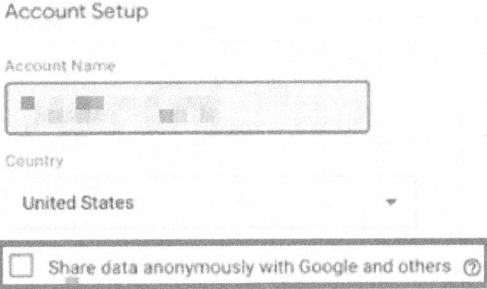

> **Container Setup**: Fill out the container name field with your primary domain, Remove the prefix "https://" from your domain, and choose "web" as your target platform. Then, click on the "create" button.

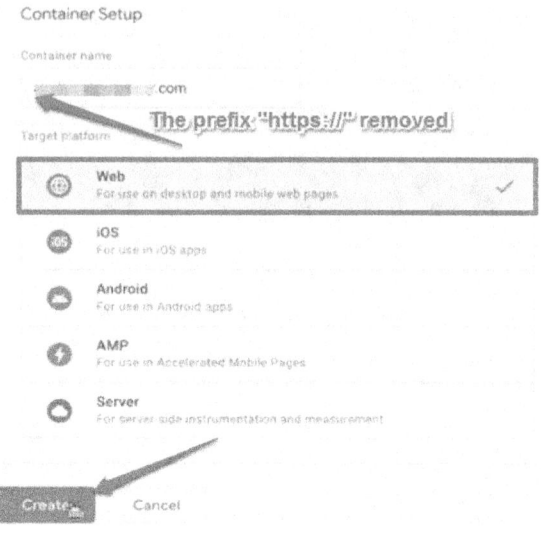

❖ The terms of service for Google Tag Manager will be shown to you. Click "Yes" in the right top corner after checking the square box to indicate your agreement.

❖ Then, you will be taken to your Google Tag Manager workspace, where a code will be provided for you to copy and paste into your website. Before adding the header and body tags to your website, copy and paste them into a notepad or any other available source on your PC.

Perhaps you closed the presented code by mistake. To retrieve it, go to the top of the page and click on your container ID.

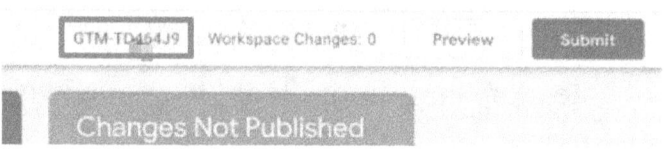

Next, I'll outline how to install Google Tag Manager on your WordPress website.

How to Install Google Tag Manager on your WordPress website

❖ On the dashboard of your WordPress website, select the "Plugin" tab from the "Settings" menu, then click on "Add New."

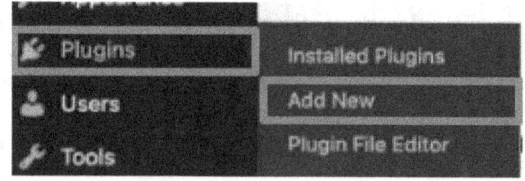

❖ Enter "Google" in the search box. Then click "Install" and then "Activate" after choosing "Site Kit by Google."

❖ Click the "Start setup" button once it has been activated.

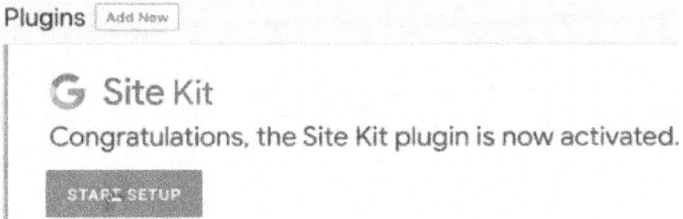

❖ Uncheck the box, then click the "Sign in with Google" button.

Set up Site Kit

Get insights on how people find your site, as well as how to improve and m

uncheck the box

Help us improve Site Kit by sharing anonymous usage data.
All collected data is treated in accordance with the Google Privacy Policy.

SIGN IN WITH GOOGLE

❖ You'll then log in using the Gmail account or email address you provided when registering for Google Tag Manager.

❖ Click on "continue" after checking these boxes.

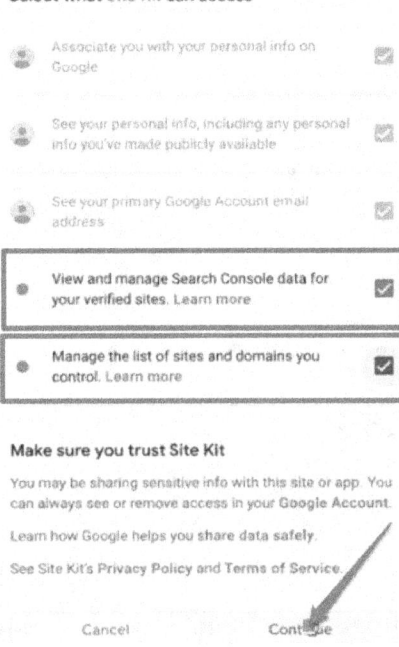

Select what Site Kit can access

Associate you with your personal info on Google ☑

See your personal info, including any personal info you've made publicly available ☑

See your primary Google Account email address ☑

View and manage Search Console data for your verified sites. Learn more ☑

Manage the list of sites and domains you control. Learn more ☑

Make sure you trust Site Kit

You may be sharing sensitive info with this site or app. You can always see or remove access in your Google Account.

Learn how Google helps you share data safely.

See Site Kit's Privacy Policy and Terms of Service.

Cancel   Continue

❖ Click on the "Proceed" button.

1 Verify site ownership

Let's verify your ownership of � �a▄▄▄▄▄▄▄▄▄▄▄▄▄▄. We'll need to upload a verification HTML file to your site.

Proceed   Cancel

2 Allow ▄▄▄▄▄▄▄▄▄▄▄▄▄ to access Google Account data.

3 Set up Search Console

❖ Then, click on the "Allow" button.

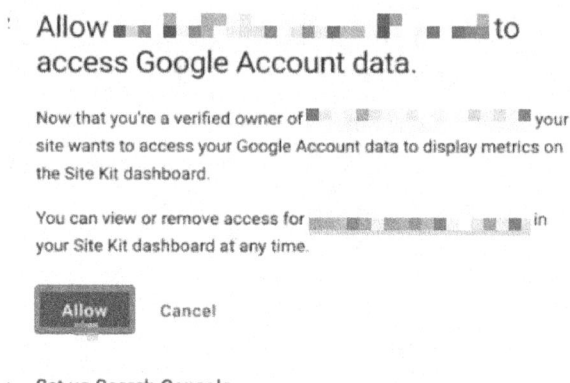

❖ Click on the "Add site" button.

G Welcome to Site Kit! Let's get you set up

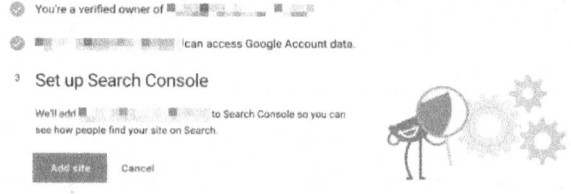

❖ Go ahead and click the "Go to my Dashboard" button.

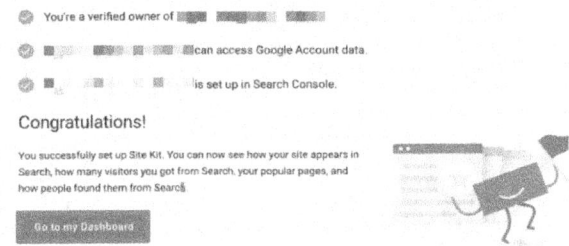

❖ This confirmation page will appear on your WordPress website dashboard to let you know that Site Kit has been successfully installed. Click "Ok, I got it" to confirm.

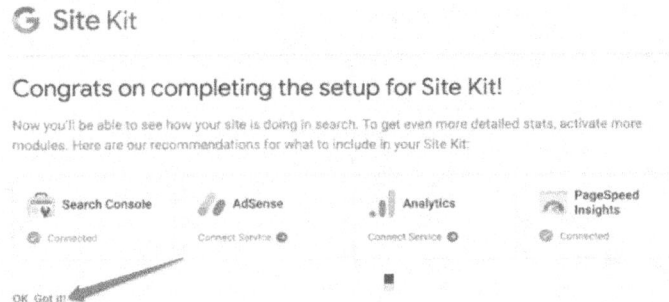

❖ Go to "settings" on your WordPress website dashboard and select "Connect more services."

❖ Click "Set up Tag Manager" under "Tag Manager" after scrolling down the page.

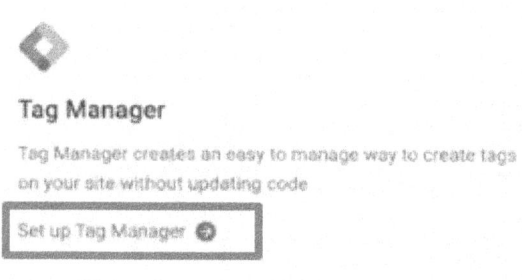

❖ Even though you have already set up your account, you must still click the "Continue" button to confirm it once more by signing in again with the same registered Gmail or email address.

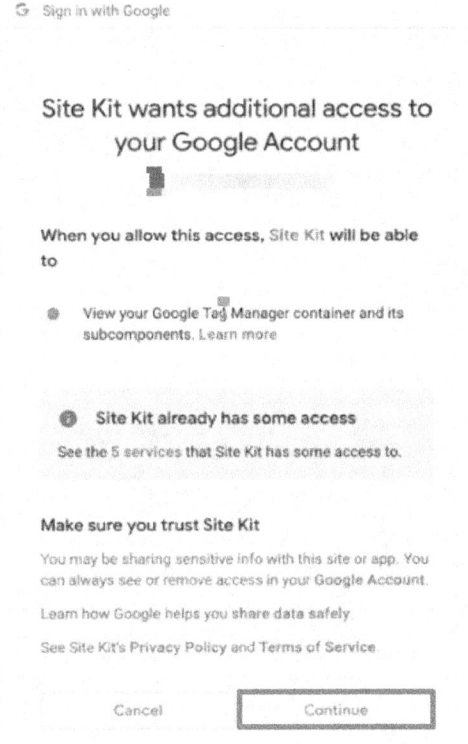

❖ You will be taken to a page similar to this one, where you can choose your account from the drop-down menu in the box. Your container name will already be selected by default. Click on the "confirm and continue" button.

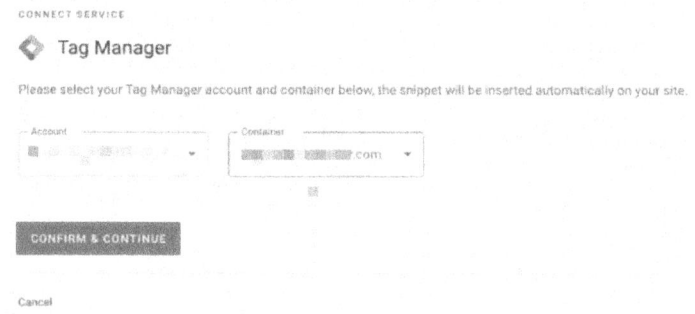

Finally, Google Tag Manager is set up on your WordPress website.

How to check if Google Tag Manager has been installed on your website.

I'll mention two Google-owned extensions so you can check if Google Tag Manager has been set up on your website. They are as follows:

    a. Google Tag Assistant

    b. Tag Assistant Legacy

I'll outline the procedures for using Tag Assistant Legacy as follows:

❖ The goal of this extension is to be installed inside your Chrome extension browser, so open your Chrome browser and type "Google Tag Assistant Chrome Extension."

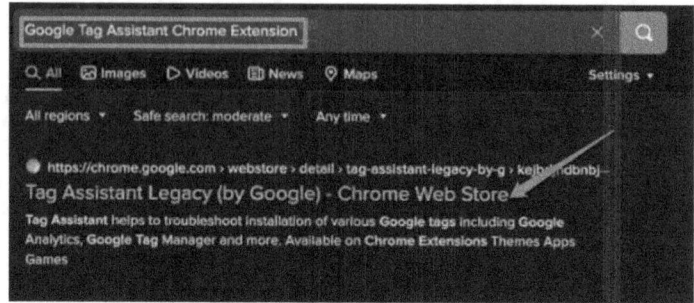

❖ Add it to your extension and authorize the installation.

❖ When the "Add to Chrome" button is clicked, a pop-up window will appear in the right corner of the page; simply click the "Done" button.

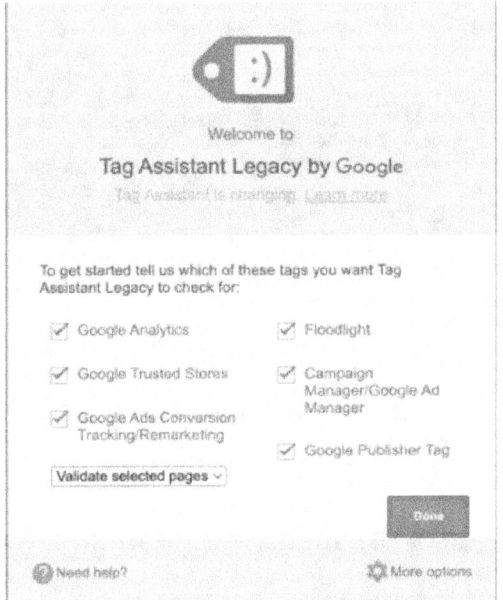

❖ Make sure you pin the extension you have installed, or you can choose to enable it so that whenever you open the page of the website you are tracking, it will display its activities.

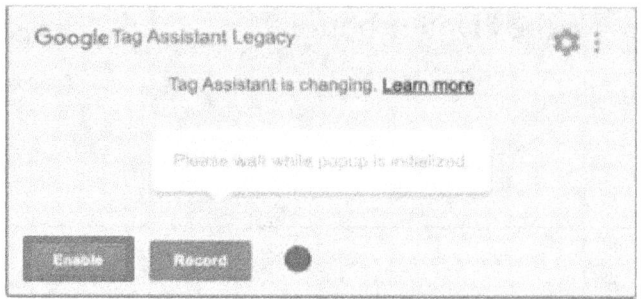

❖ When you click on the icon at the top of your browser, if the website you are tracking is already open and the extension is enabled, it will look like this, which will also include the container ID of your Google Tag Manager.

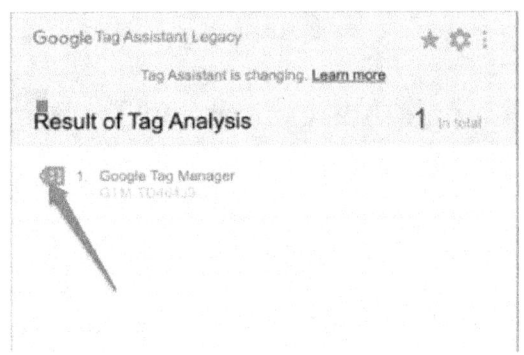

Note: *"Blue or green" in front of Google Tag Manager denotes proper setup, as the arrow in the image above indicates. If the display indicates "yellow" or "red," it simply means there are some errors or the installation was unsuccessful.*

Chapter 7

Google Ads Conversion Tracking

I will list two ways for you to track your confirmation or thank you page as a conversion, but I will only explain one way to do so. They are:

1. Through Shopify Help Center

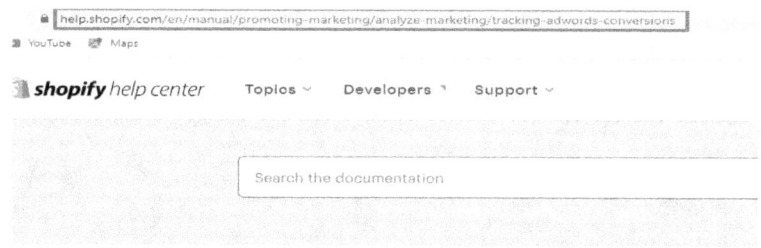

They are entirely based on Google Ads conversion tracking.

2. Through WooCommerce Plugin

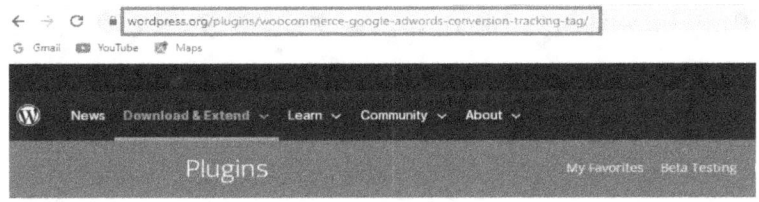

You can easily set up your conversion tracking on your website by using the WooCommerce Pixel Manager plugin.

The steps below will show you how to track your website's thank-you page as a conversion after your visitors have entered their information in the provided opt-in form. I'll discuss a chrome extension you can use to see if all the events on your thank you page were tracked because Google conversion tracking is so extensive that the data won't be displayed on the Google Ads interface.

❖ Setup your conversion tracking goal by choosing "conversion" from the list of options under "Tools and settings" at the top of the interface page for your Google Ads All campaign or expert mode.

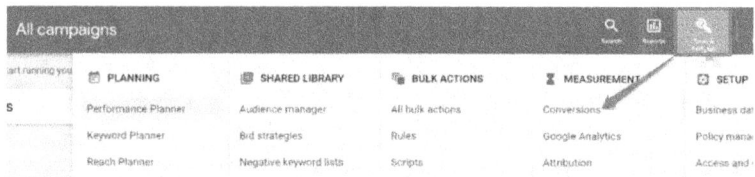

❖ Under Conversion Actions, click on the "+" button.

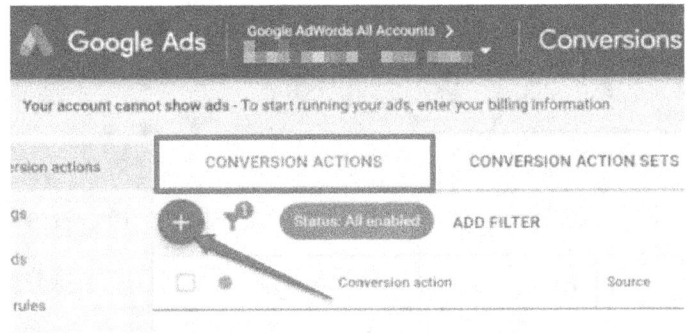

❖ Choose a website because we'll be using it.

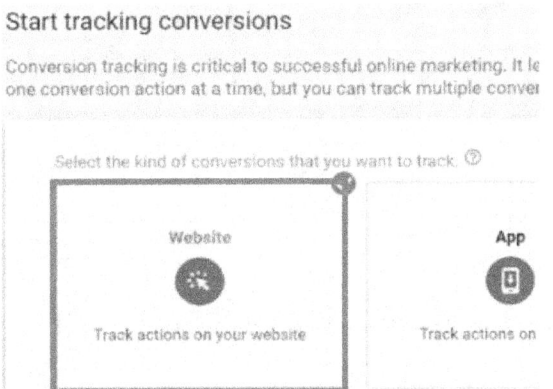

❖ On the first phase, "create a conversion action for your website,"

➤ **Category**: Choose a category that fits the goal you are tracking. I want to track people who subscribe to my email list through my landing page. I must therefore choose an option that is in line with my goal. So I'll choose "Sign up" from the drop-down menu.

➤ **Conversion name**: I'll give it a name that matches my landing page. i.e: sign-up-booth. Always rely on what you can recall.

➢ Value

★ Use the same value for each conversion: Here, you will enter how much each conversion is worth to you. You'll enter the currency and amount.

★ Use different values for each conversion: Your value may be different based on ups and downs in sales. Then, you can enter any average amount.

★ Don't use a value for this conversion action (not recommended): If you want to play it safe but not convert, you can select the option, which I won't advise you to do.

Value

Measure the impact of your advertising by giving conversions a value

◉ Use the same value for each conversion
Each time a conversion happens, the same value is recorded

Enter the value that should be used for this conversion action

US Dollar (USD $) ∨ 1

○ Use different values for each conversion

○ Don't use a value for this conversion action (not recommended)

➢ Count

★ Every: If you are selling different items, you can track every single sale of those items for each person for whom the person signs up on different lists.

★ One: Also, you can decide to track only one person if the person signs up and can buy enough products. Then we count it as just one conversion.

This depends on you and the nature of your products.

> **Conversion Window**

★ Click-through conversion window: This is the number of days that will count after somebody clicks on your ad. Setting it for higher days will be okay. If you set it to 30 days, that will not be considered a conversion. 90 is the maximum number of days, even if you choose a custom option.

For example, if you are selling a pencil and somebody forgot to see your ad for a month, there are chances to see it after the days pass because people mostly take their time to research some products. Setting the number to be higher is the best idea, and it makes more sense so that people will take more time to research that particular product you're running ads for.

Click-through conversion window

Conversions can happen days after a perso the maximum time after an ad interaction th conversions ⑦

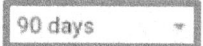

★ Engaged-view conversion window: This is mostly for video views; assuming someone has seen at least 10 seconds of your video and you want to give them 3 days after they sign up for your list, that will be considered a conversion. Any action after the stated days won't be considered a conversion.

Engaged-view conversion window   Select how long to track conversions after a v

★ View-through conversion window: This counts the time between actual impressions of your ad; if somebody clicks but still sees your ad, then it will be recorded as a conversion. Assuming somebody sees your ad and may buy your products a few days later, setting it to 3 days is okay for me, and you may probably set it to the days you prefer depending on the business you do and the service you are rendering.

View-through conversion window   Select the maximum time after a person views your ad that you want to count view-through conversions ⑦

➢ **Check the Include in "conversion" column**. This will show every single conversion you've set up. Meaning that for all the processes I have explained earlier, you can repeat them for other conversions like purchase, up-sell, and down-sell or whatever you are tracking. It simply means that when you check this column, all of them will be included in "conversion."

Include in 'Conversions'   ☑ Include these conversions in your 'Conversions' column. If you use conver they will optimise for these conversions ⑦

➢ **Attribution Model**: The drop-down menu includes the last click, first click, linear, time decay, position-based, and data-driven. We select the default which is the last click.

★ Last click: Assuming you have different ads, like display ads, YouTube ads, and search ads, people might see all these ads. When you select "last click" from the drop-down menu, it means the last type of ad people see, it may be a YouTube ad, which will be the ad that will get credited for that sale. The other two (display and search ads) will not see conversions. This also applies to the "first click" option if it is selected.

★ Linear: It means if you make a sale and people saw all three ads, then each of them will have one-third of the credit, i.e.,

0.33, 0.33, 0.34 of the conversion in the column for every single one of those ads.

★ Time decay: It means that the first ad will still get some conversion credits but not as much as the last ad

★ Position-based: It means the first and last ad will get the most credit, while other ads will get half of what they got.

★ Data-driven: This is generally the best option because Google will use the whole algorithm to figure out which ad contributed to the sale. You need at least 100 conversions for the options to be used; lots of conversions are advised for this option.

Select an attribution model for your conversions ⑦

The attribution model determines how much credit each ad interaction get

....| Last click ▾

➢ **Deselect the "Enable Enhanced CPC"** because Google will charge you more beyond your bid settings. Then, click on "create and continue"

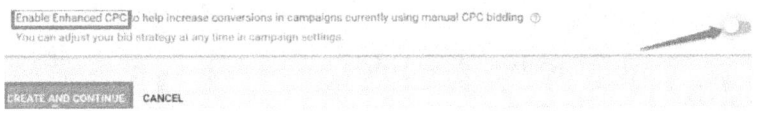

Enable Enhanced CPC to help increase conversions in campaigns currently using manual CPC bidding ⑦

You can adjust your bid strategy at any time in campaign settings.

CREATE AND CONTINUE   CANCEL

❖ "Tag setup" is the second phase. Three options will be presented to you for adding the tag to your website: "Install the tag yourself," "Email the tag," and "use Google Tag Manager." Choose "Install the tag yourself" from the options.

You've created a conversion action. Now, set up the tag to add to your website.

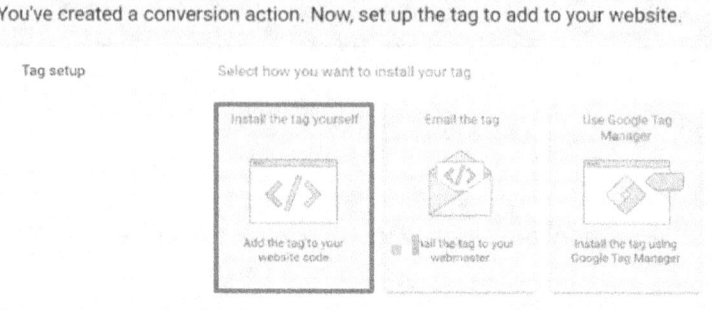

You will scroll down the page after choosing this option to find two codes that need to be installed;

> **Base Code**: This will be added to every page of your website.

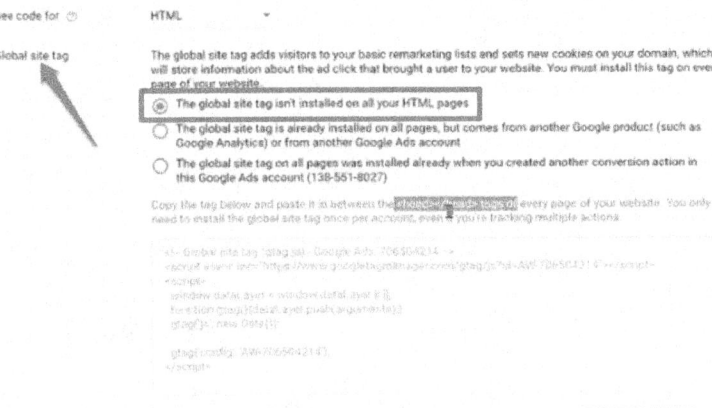

> **Event Code**: You'll use this code to track specific events. In other words, you will track those who subscribe to your opt-in list. Additionally, you'll add the event code specifically to the thank-you page because only those who subscribe to your list will be able to access it, serving as proof that they have indeed done so.

On each page of your website, add the base code between the head></head> tags.

I mentioned a plugin like Site Kit by Google that you can use if you have a WordPress website.

You want to track people's activity after pasting the event code onto the specific page. Then, click the "Next" button.

❖ Click on the "Done" button. You will have to wait a short while before Google verifies your conversion tracking.

❖ You must download and install a Chrome extension called Tag Assistant Legacy (by Google) on your Chrome browser to confirm that the codes were added correctly. Finally, pin the extension you've installed.

❖ Refresh your landing page and thank you page.Then, click on the extension; if the

code has been properly set up, you should
be able to see something similar to this.

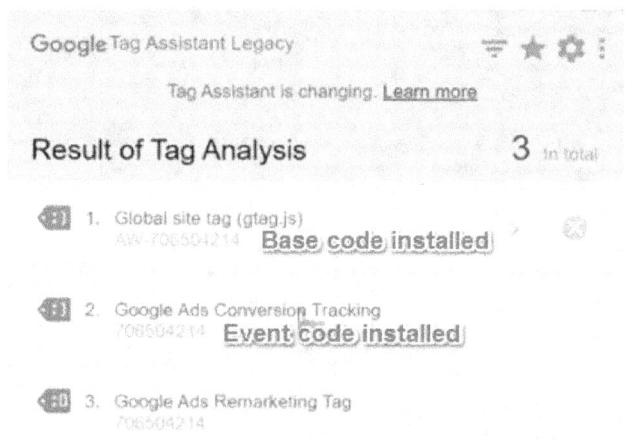

How to track conversions using Google Ads and
Google Tag Manager will be covered in detail in
the next section

How to track Conversion with Google Ads and Google Tag Manager

Follow the instructions I provided earlier on "Google Ads Conversion Tracking." I will then begin at Step VIII.

❖ In the second phase, "set up the tag," Three options will be presented to you for adding the tag to your website: "Install the tag yourself," "Email the tag," and "use Google Tag Manager." Choose "Use Google Tag Manager" from the options.

❖ To track your new conversion in Google Tag Manager, you'll receive a conversion ID and label. You'll need to use them, so copy them.

❖ Click the "New" button in the right corner of the "Tags" section on your GTM dashboard.

❖ Give the tag a name, click "Tag configuration," and then from the list of choices, choose "Google Ads conversion tracking."

❖ If you see the message "Conversion Linker Tag missing in container" on the Google Ads conversion tracking interface, click the "create" button, give the tag a name, and then click "save."

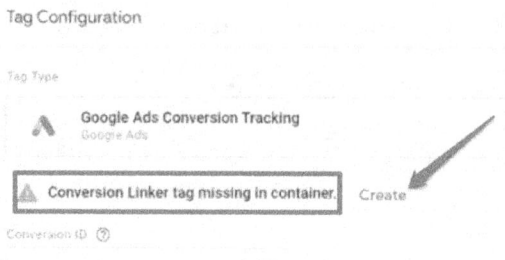

Insert the conversion ID and label that you copied in Step II. Don't worry about entering the conversion value, transaction ID, and currency code into the spaces provided.

❖ You must include "trigger" in the tag. Select "trigger" by clicking. A new trigger can be created, or an existing trigger can be chosen. I will choose "Email Sign Up" since I already have a trigger for the conversion action I wanted to track. Next, click the "save" button, and then click the "submit" button.

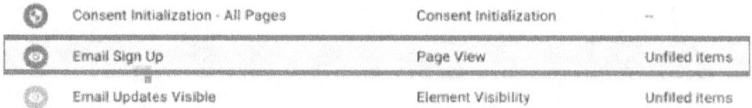

❖ Give it a version name and click the "Publish" button.

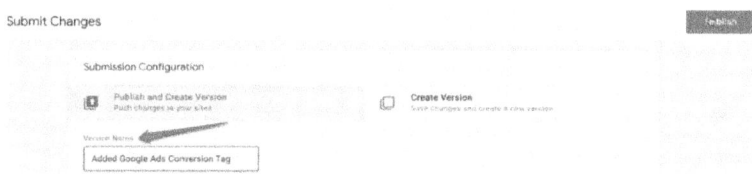

Your website is now linked to the Google Ads conversion tag.

Chapter 8

Google Analytics

Google Analytics is a web analytics service that offers data and fundamental analytical tools for marketing and search engine optimization (SEO) needs. Anyone with a Google account can access the service, which is a component of the Google Marketing Platform, without charge.

It is employed to track website performance and gather visitor insights. Organizations can use it to identify the main user traffic sources, evaluate the effectiveness of their marketing initiatives and campaigns, track goal accomplishments like purchases and cart additions, identify patterns and trends in user engagement, and gather other visitor data like demographics. Numerous customer behavior analytics can be obtained and analyzed using Google Analytics by small and medium-sized retail websites. These analytics can be used to enhance marketing campaigns, increase website traffic, and better retain visitors.

How does Google Analytics function?

By using page tags, Google Analytics collects user information from each person who visits a website. Every page's code contains a JavaScript page tag. Every time a visitor accesses the website, this tag runs in their web browser, gathering information and sending it to a Google data collection server. Then, Google Analytics can produce tailored reports to monitor and display information such as user counts, bounce rates, typical session lengths, sessions by channel, page views, goal completions, and more.

Features of Google Analytics

Google Analytics has tools that can be used to help users spot patterns and trends in how people interact with their websites. Features make it possible to collect data, analyze it, monitor it, display it, generate reports, and integrate it with other applications. They consist of the following:

1. Dashboards, scorecards, and motion charts that show changes in data over time are examples of data visualization and monitoring tools.
2. Data manipulation, filtering, and funnel analysis.
3. APIs for application programs that collect data.

4. Anomaly detection, intelligence, and predictive analytics.

5. segmentation for subset analytics, such as conversion analytics.

6. Customized audience behavior, advertising, acquisition, and conversion reports.

7. communication and sharing via email, and

8. integration with additional products such as Google Ads, Google Data Studio, Salesforce Marketing Cloud, Google Adsense, Google Optimize 360, Google Display and Video 360, Google Ad Manager, and Google Search Console.

The Google Analytics dashboard allows users to save profiles for multiple websites and view details for pre-defined categories or choose custom metrics to display for each website.

Overviews of the content, keywords, referring websites, visitors, map overlays, and traffic sources are just a few of the categories that can be tracked.

The dashboard is accessible via a widget or plugin for embedding into other websites and can be viewed on the Google Analytics website. Additional options for customized Google Analytics dashboards come from unaffiliated vendors.

Important Google Analytics metrics

A metric is a benchmark for a numerical measurement. Users of Google Analytics can monitor up to 200 different metrics to evaluate the effectiveness of their websites. Even though some metrics might be more important to some businesses than others, these are some of the most well-liked ones:

1. Users: A user is a unique or first-time website visitor.
2. Sessions: a 30-minute period of time during which some visitor interactions take place.
3. Average session duration: the average amount of time each visitor spends on the website.
4. Bounce rate: the proportion of visitors who only viewed one page. The Google Analytics server received just one request from these visitors.
5. Percentage of new sessions: The proportion of website visits that are brand-new visits

6. Goal completions: The number of times visitors carry out a desired action that is specified. Another name for this is a conversion.

7. Page views: The total number of pages that have been viewed.

8. Pages per session: The typical number of pages viewed in a session

Advantages of Google Analytics

The following advantages are offered by Google Analytics:

1. Quick web insights and access to custom reports

2. Statistical and reporting software

3. Customizable metrics and dimensions

4. Combines with different platforms and tools

5. Free service, easy to use and beginner friendly

Google Tag Manager and Google Analytics

Your life can be greatly simplified by having both of these tools. You can transfer data from Google Tag Manager to Google Analytics so that you can examine it, spot trends, and have all the information you require in one location. To see which links are being downloaded by users or for pretty much any other purpose you might want to gather data for, it is simple to set up by using a click trigger and a tag from Google Analytics. To send the data to Google Analytics automatically, the triggers can also be used to choose specific times. However, when used together, these two tools can be even more beneficial.

Google Analytics 4 (GA4), the most recent version of the software, gives you access to the most recent version of Google Analytics if you follow the instructions for setting up your account.

Steps for setting up Google Analytics Account
The steps listed below describe how to create and configure your Google Analytics account.

- ❖ To get started, type "Google Analytics" into the search bar on your computer to sign up. You'll then see a page similar to this one; click "Sign up." Click "create an account" to continue if you're using a mobile device.

   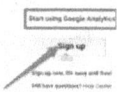

❖ The Admin interface requires you to enter your account name, website name, URL, industry category, and reporting time zone. Any name, including the name of your company, is acceptable for your account. Click "Get Tracking ID" once you're done.

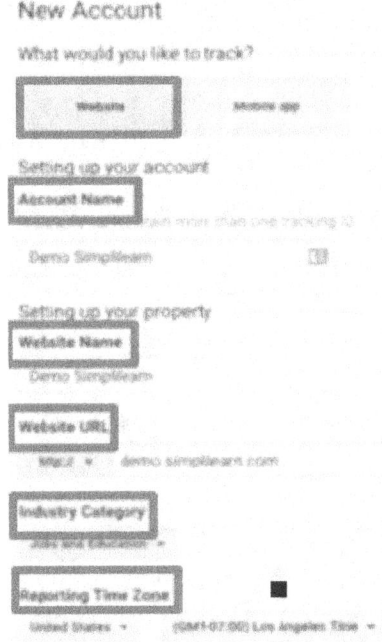

❖ Accept the terms of service for Google Analytics. Choose "I accept"

❖ You will be brought to the user interface, where you can copy the tracking code and see your tracking ID. The tracking ID always has the following format: UA-xxxxxxxx-1, where -1 is the number of properties set up. If you want to track multiple websites on the same account, you must set up multiple properties. For example, if you set up three properties in your account, you will either have -1, -2, or -3 properties, depending on how many you set up.

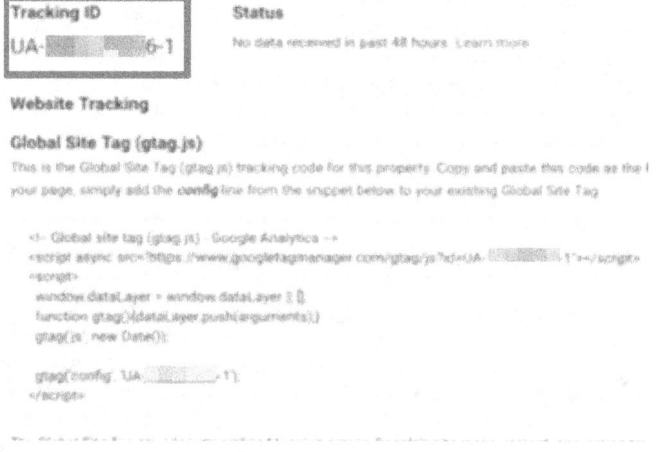

Note: *Over time, software upgrades may cause the interface for creating an account for this tool to change.*

Chapter 9

Google Analytics 4 (GA4)

The newest version of this service, referred to as Google Analytics 4 or GA4, was made available in October 2020. Google Analytics earlier iterations have undergone some changes with GA4. It provides a completely new user interface and switches from using third-party cookies to using machine learning for more accurate data collection.

The new features in Google Analytics 4 include the following:

- ❖ Tools for artificial intelligence (AI) and machine learning
- ❖ Enhanced Google Ads integration

❖ Customer-focused reporting built based on lifecycle data

❖ Extra codeless tracking capabilities that can deliver data with lower latency; and

❖ Improved data control features for data management and regulatory compliance

How to use Google Tag Manager and Google Analytics 4 to track Google Ads conversions.

❖ Go to the GTM website, as indicated in the highlighted image below, to create your free account as I described in the preceding step.

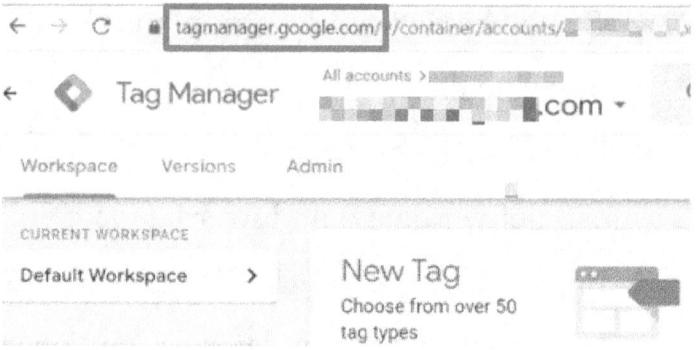

❖ Following the creation of your free account, the first action you should take is to click the "Admin" button on the GTM dashboard and then "Install Google Tag Manager."

❖ Add a snippet to your website by copying and pasting. The first is placed between your website's head> tag and the opening body> tag, while the second comes right after. For instructions on how to do it, refer to the previous setup on GTM. Return to your Google Tag Manager Workspace dashboard once you have finished the setup.

❖ Click "Add a new Tag" under the New Tag section on your GTM dashboard.

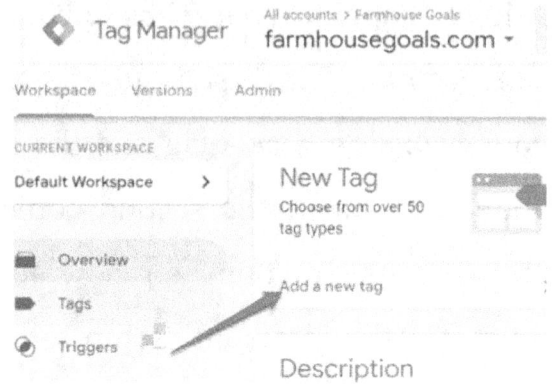

❖ After naming the tag as "Google Analytics 4", click on Tag configuration and select "Google Analytics: GA4 Configuration" from the list of available tag options.

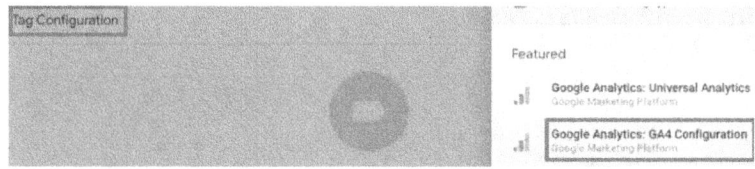

❖ You must enter your measurement ID in the designated field on this "Google Analytics: GA4 Configuration" interface.

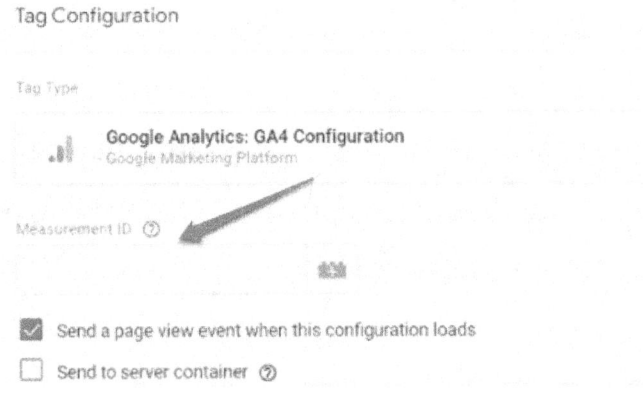

❖ You can obtain the measurement ID directly by logging into your Google Analytics account, going to the "Admin" section, and clicking on "Setup Assistant," which is the first link on the property.

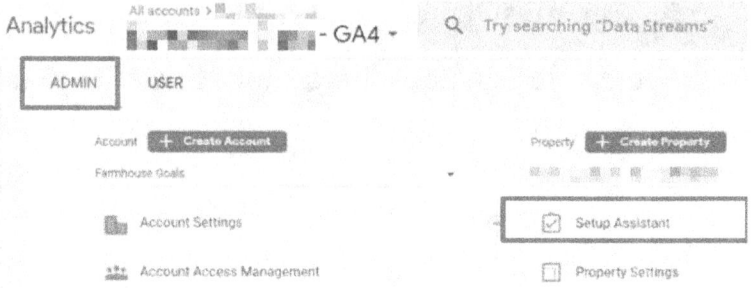

> Click on the "Tag Installation" arrow under "collection" on the Setup Assistant interface.

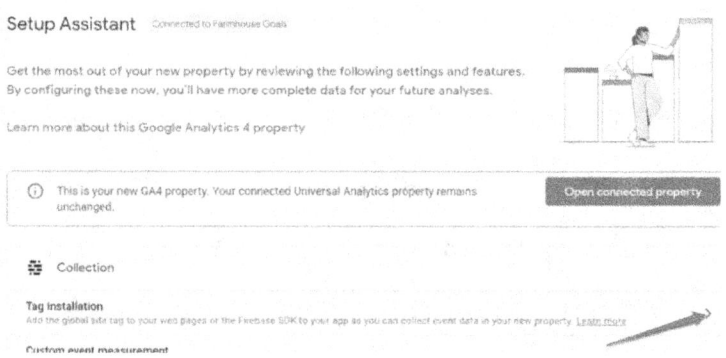

➤ You'll be directed to the "Data Streams" page. Select your data stream by clicking on it.

➤ You'll be able to see your measurement ID. Then copy it

i.e., Admin > Setup Assistant > Collection > Tag Installation > Data Streams > Measurements ID.

❖ Go back to GTM and then enter the copied measurement ID into the empty field in step VI. Nothing needs to be changed other than simply pasting the ID. Scroll down and select "Triggering"

❖ You must include "trigger" in the tag. Click on "triggering" and select "All Pages." Click on "save" and submit the changes by clicking on the "submit" button.

❖ After submitting the changes, give the version a name and include any optional version descriptions you desire. Click on

"Publish." Google Analytics 4 and Google Tag Manager are now linked.

❖ The next step is to add the GA4 tag to your website. Click "Add a new tag" under "New Tag" in the GTM workspace. Name the tag "Google Analytics." Next, click on tag configuration and choose "Google Analytics: Universal Analytics" from the list of Google tags.

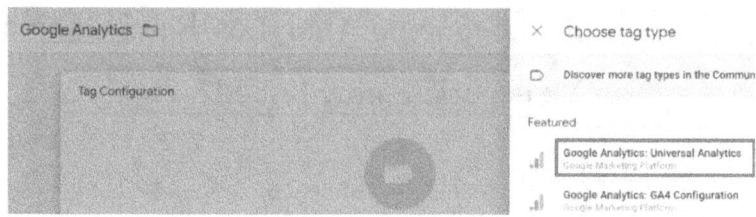

❖ Keep your track type set to "Page View" in the "Google Analytics: Universal Analytics" interface. Select "New variable" in Google Analytics settings.

➤ You will be prompted to enter your tracking ID here. Your Google Analytics tracking ID is what you need.

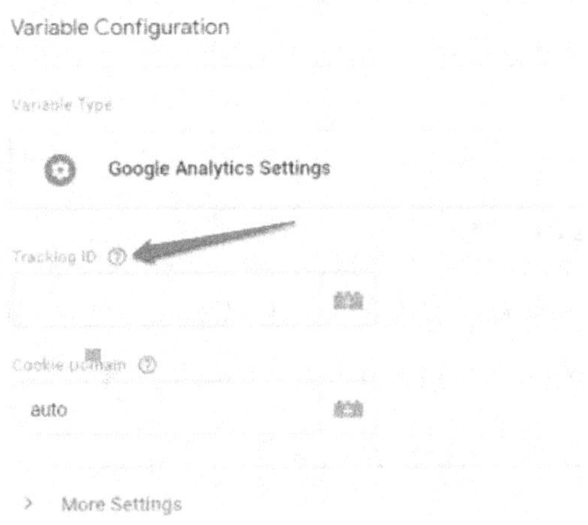

Variable Configuration

Variable Type

⊙ Google Analytics Settings

Tracking ID ⑦

Cookie Domain ⑦

auto

> More Settings

❖ Return to your Google Analytics account, click on "property settings," and then copy your tracking ID. Then click on "save." That will be a new variable for your tag configuration.

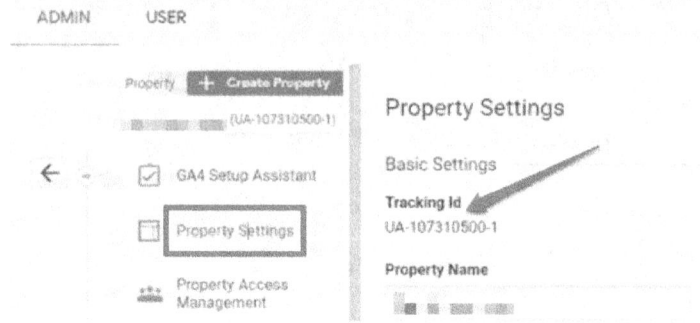

❖ You must include "trigger" in the tag. Scroll down by clicking on "triggering" and selecting "All Pages." For the changes to be submitted, click "Save."

You can see that Google Analytics 4 has been added, along with variables and tags, when you view your workspace changes. Click the "Submit" button.

Workspace Changes

Name ↑	Type	Change	Last Edited
GA Settings	Variable	Added	a few seconds ago
Google Analytics New	Tag	Added	a few seconds ago

Note: *Keep in mind that you don't need to install Universal Analytics if you are using GA4.*

❖ Give it a version name, submit changes for your setup, and click on "Publish."

How to use Google Analytics 4 to track Google Ads conversions.

❖ Go to your GA4 account. You can create your event directly from your Google Analytics 4 account or choose to use any already-existing event by clicking the "configure" tab on the page's vertical left side. Click the "create event" button to start a new event.

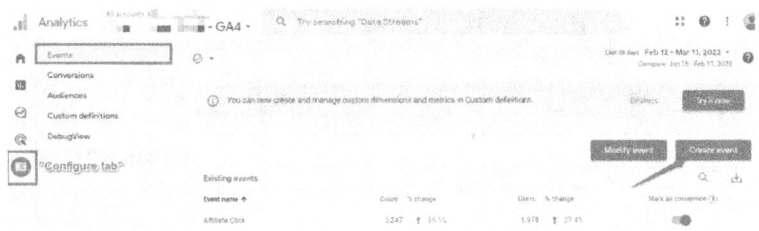

❖ I've already created an event with the name "generate_lead." I'll click on it to edit, or you can click the "create" button to add a new event.

❖ Give your configuration a name, specify your value (the name of the URL destination page), and specify a condition for the confirmation page or any other destination page you want to use to track events. You can also include multiple conditions in your settings. In the top right corner of the page, select the "create" button.

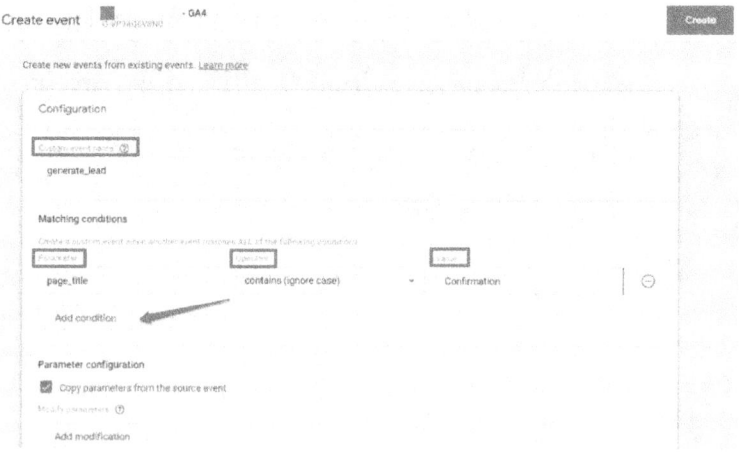

The "generate_lead" event name I recently created simply denotes the fact that each time someone accesses the confirmation page (value), it will be recorded as an "event," which functions exactly like

GTM, with the exception that I'm doing it through my GA4 account directly.

❖ After creating an event, select "conversion" from the configure tab menu on your GA4 account. By selecting the "New conversion event" button, I will create a new conversion with the same event name as my previous one, "generate_lead." Then, click on "save"

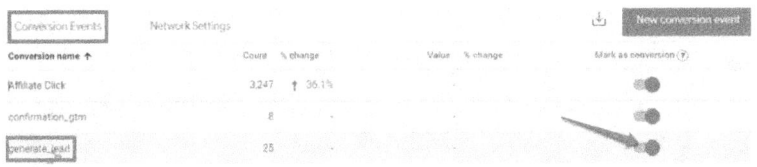

❖ Return to your Google Ad account and select "Tools and settings." From the drop-down menu under "measurement," click on "conversion."

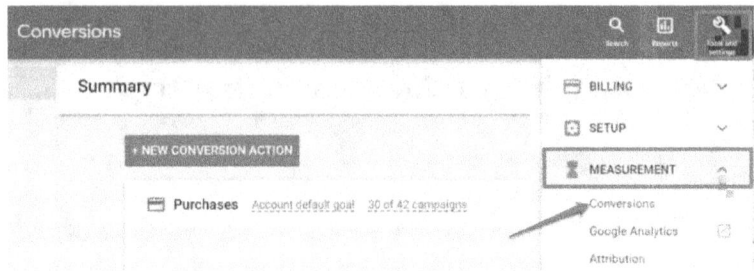

❖ Click "+ New Conversion" once more. Choose "Import" from the list of 4 options.

Choose "Google Analytics 4 properties." Click the "Continue" button after selecting "Web" from the list of options.

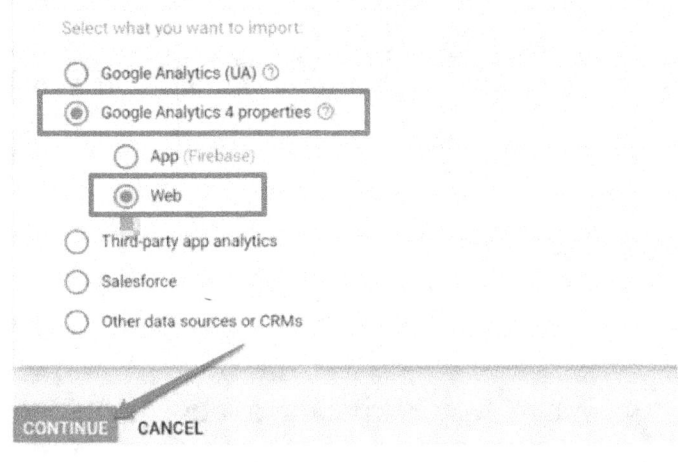

❖ You must choose which conversion actions to import from the Google Analytics 4 property on the following page. i.e: "generate_lead" As a result of your successful configuration, this will be displayed automatically. The "Import" and "Continue" buttons should be clicked after checking the box.

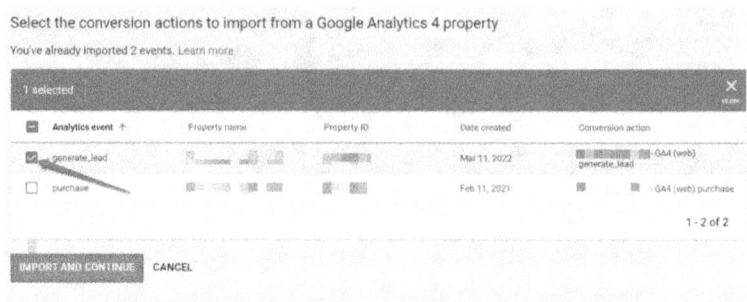

Select the conversion actions to import from a Google Analytics 4 property

❖ When you arrive at a new page, it will inform you that a web conversion action from GA4 has been imported. Click on the "Done" button.

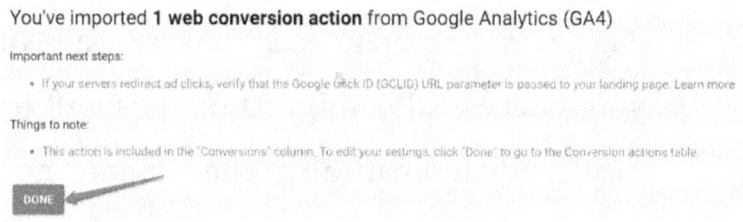

You've imported **1 web conversion action** from Google Analytics (GA4)

You can edit your created conversion settings, such as goal, value, count, etc., under "summary."

Conclusion

With Google Ads, qualified, in-market prospects can be targeted at a low cost. If managed effectively, Google Ads can generate a significant return on investment while helping you boost leads and sales for your business. Even if your SEO strategy has given you a strong online presence, research shows that incorporating Google Ads advertising increases the number of search clicks by a significant amount.

Since Google Ads first launched more than 18 years ago, the price of advertising has skyrocketed. People who have been around since those early days recall $0.01 clicks. Consider yourself fortunate if you only pay ten times that amount today.

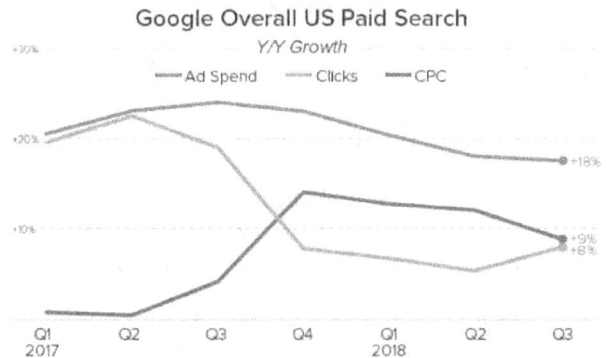

Rise in Google Ads CPC - Source: Merkle Q3 2018 Statistics

Google Ads users have improved over time by becoming more knowledgeable, learning what works and what doesn't, and changing their strategy. They have a significant advantage over stores that are new to the platform because of this. Therefore, you must be at your best if you hope to compete with them profitably. The opportunity to experiment and try new things on your own is frequently very limited.

So what can you do to begin using Google Ads right away? Here are my top recommendations:

1. Make use of automation

It takes a long time to become proficient in Google Ads. The good news is that you don't have to start learning everything right away. With its "Google Shopping" form of advertising, Google automates the majority of labor-intensive tasks.

Once you've created a product feed from your store, Google Shopping will match your products to relevant search queries.

2. Begin modestly

Don't launch your advertising campaign for all of your products at once if you sell hundreds of them. To give yourself some room for error, pick a class of products or a market where your margins are higher.

Additionally, fewer products will lower the total cost. Because it's preferable to keep your expenses in check as long as you're not completely certain of what you're doing. Then, as orders begin to come in and the numbers start to make sense, gradually expand the range of the products you're advertising.

3. Get wiser

Learning a new skill always requires time. Fortunately, you are not the first. The most efficient way to learn is by doing. Therefore, familiarize yourself with how to improve those results if you're launching your first campaign with a limited number of products.

4. Get professional assistance

Some agencies and freelancers have specialized in Google Ads for many years. They are unable to predict the future, but if they have enough experience, they are likely to have worked with or in your industry previously.

Additionally, it might be difficult to generate sales with Google Ads if you don't lay the proper groundwork. Therefore, if you claim that Google Ads don't work for you, one of these three factors is usually to blame:

5. Average order value

You won't have any money left over to pay for expensive clicks if your average order value is too low. If each click costs $0.5, selling a $6 product cannot be profitable.

6. Margins

This is associated with the average order value. There won't be any money left over to invest in advertising if your gross margins are too low or if your average order value is low but your margins are high.

7. Conversion rate

Your conversion rate must be comparable to your competitors' since you are paying similar CPCs. Otherwise, you risk being easily outspent by competitors.

These are not unbreakable laws. However, using Google Ads will be challenging if your company experiences any of the aforementioned problems.

www.ingramcontent.com/pod-product-compliance
Lightning Source LLC
Chambersburg PA
CBHW071135220526
45467CB00015B/1080